The Largest Water Control Project in the World

Three Gorges Project in China

Chief editor: Lu Jin

CHANGJIANG PRESS

Dream is Coming True (Preface)

Originating from the southwest side of Geladandong Snow Mountain, the highest peak of the Tangula Mountains on the Qinghai-Tibet Plateau (known as the "Top of the world"), the Yangtze River converges hundreds of rivers , streams and creeks flowing through 11 provinces, municipalities and autonomous regions in China, the Yangtze River is 6300km in full length with a catchment area of 1,800,000km2, accounting for one fifth of the total area in the country and people in this area create 40% of the wealth in the country. The Yangtze River is the largest river in China and the third largest river in the world.

The Yangtze River came into being about 200 million years ago. Like the Yellow River, it is both the cradle for the Chinese nation and the place Chinese ancient culture originated. With the advent of the new century, the Yangtze River exhibits energy, vitality, enthusiasm and glory everywhere, and stands in the east world with its charming posture and grand air. The Chinese people are accomplishing a grand project in the Three Gorges on the Yangtze River, which provides robust power for the grand renaissance of the Chinese nation .

On June 1, 2003, the world-known Three Gorges Project began impounding water initially. Within a short time of 10 days, fundamental changes took place to the whole Three Gorges, turning it into a huge man-made lake in the world. On June 16, the dual-channel and five-step permanent ship lock for the Three Gorges Project was put into trial navigation. In June, the first generating units of the Three Gorges Project started to generate power and connected into power grid, indicating that the Three Gorges Project had entered its initial harvest period through extensive efforts in the past decade.

The Three Gorges Project has taken 70 years for conception, 50 years for research and 30 years for demonstration. The dream is eventually coming true! It is 86 years since the initiation of the Three Gorges Project dream by Sun Yat-sen in 1919. In near a century, the Three Gorges Project has attracted extensive attention from so many important figures, triggered extensive demonstration and left a lot of touching stories. The Three Gorges Project changes the grand Three Gorges, the masterpiece of nature, and reservoir impoundment raises its water level to EL.175m, thus creating a huge reservoir with a storage capacity of 39.3 billio cubic meters.

Undoubtedly, we now have a clear picture in mind about th great expectation the Three Gorges Project brings for the Ch nese nation! Indeed, the Chinese people have long dreamed the Three Gorges Project! Faced with frequent occurrence floodhazards in China, we cannot depend on countless civil peopl and military forces to resist rampant flood with their bodies yea after year. When China is in urgent need of energy sources fo her renaissance today, we cannot bear to see the substantia potential energy contained by the Yangtze River flow away with out being used. At a historic moment when the development West China and Yangtze River Economic Belt decides China future destiny, we cannot bear to see the Yangtze River waterwa that cuts through Central China and West China slow down he pace just because of natural obstructions at the Three Gorges This is why the Chinese people have dreamed of the Three Gorge Project for a century and eventually turned this dream into reality Witnessing the dramatic changes to the Three Gorges on th Yangtze River, it is our obligatory duty to record these great event in these albums.

The Chinese people have dreamed of the Three Gorge Project for a century but when this dream comes true eventually the lovely homestead we have long lived in has become our by gone dream. It is really a pity that nothing in the world is satisfac tory in every aspect. Faced with today's mirror-like lake in the Three Gorges, we should feel sufficiently comfortable and satis fied that the Three Gorges has promoted her grandeur and vast ness though she has lost some primitive tranquility and profundity What's the most important, the construction of the Three Gorges Project has created a full range of new modern towns in the Three Gorges Reservoir region and enabled Three Gorges residents to get integrated into modern living at least half a century ahead o time. In addition, this has created robust power for China to ac complish her renaissance. Let's express our benediction to the Three Gorges, to Three Gorges people and to the constructors o the Three Gorges Project! Just remember: we cannot have today's Three Gorges without them!

Grand Three Gorges Project

Three Gorges Project on the Yangtze River

三峡工程
CHINA
中 Three Gorges Project
国

Contents

I Three Gorges Project on the Yangtze River 1-59

■ Grand Three Gorges Project 18-19

■ Great Events in Three Gorges Project Construction 20-21

■ Dam Site 22-23

■ Formulation of Construction Scheme for the Three Gorges Project 24-37

■ Flood Discharge Dam section for the Three Gorges Project 38-41

■ Navigation Buildings for the Three Gorges Project 42-47

■ Power Station for the Three Gorges Project 48-55

■ World Records Created by the Construction of the Three Gorges Project 56-57

■ Comparison of the World's Eight Largest Hydropower Stations 58

■ Key Parameters of the Three Gorges Project 59

II Substantial Social and Social Economic Benefits from the Three Gorges Project .. 60-71

■ Flood Control 60-63

■ Power Generation 64-67

■ Navigation 68-71

III Solutions to Major Issues for the Three Gorges Project 72-84

■ One Million Residents for Resettlement 72-75

CONTENTS

■ Sedimentation 76-77

■ Ecological and Environmental Protection 78-79

■ Geology and Earthquake 80-81

■ Threat from War 82-83

■ Source of Funds 84

■ Economical and Financial Analysis of the Project 85

IV Gezhouba Water Control Project 86-89

■ Gezhouba Water Control Project as a Part of the Three Gorges Project 86-87

■ Key Parameters of the Gezhouba Project 88-89

V Preservation of Cultural Relics around Three Gorges 90-107

■ Ancient Buildings around Three Gorges 90-97

■ Ancient Towns around Three Gorges 98-103

■ Stone Carvings around Three Gorges 103-107

VI Tourism of New Three Gorges 108-129

■ Tourism of Three Gorges 108-119

■ Key Tourist Spots around Three Gorges Reservoir 120-129

Panoramic View of the Three Gorges Project

Three Gorges Project on the Yangtze River

Three Gorges Dam Flood Discharging

Three Gorges Project on the Yangtze River

Cut through Wushan

Three Gorges Project on the Yangtze River

Mirror- like Lake in Deep Valleys

Three Gorges Project on the Yangtze River

A Wonder in Moden World

Three Gorges Project on the Yangtze River

Night Scene of Three Gorges Dam

Three Gorges Project on the Yangtze River

Grand Three Gorges Project

The Three Gorges Water Control Project on the Yangtze River is a strategic project to harness and develop the Yangtze River, integrating such benefits as flood control, power generation and navigation. The site of the Three Gorges Dam is located at Sandouping in Yichang, Hubei, about 40km from the completed Gezhouba Water Control Project. The Three Gorges Project is the largest water control project in the world today. The Three Gorges Reservoir features 175m in normal pool storage level, 39.3 billion cubic meters in total storage capacity and 22.15 billion cubic meters in effective flood control capacity, thus upgrading the flood control standard of the river section around Jingzhou to once-in-100-year standard from current once-in-10-year standard. Located on the left and right sides of the overflow dam section, hydropower stations house 26 hydropower generating units in total with 700MW in single unit capacity, 18,200MW in total installed capacity and 84.68TWh in annual power generation. The project can substantially improve the river channel from Yichang to Chongqing on the Yangtze River and 10,000 tonnage ships can directly navigate to Chongqing Port. The Three Gorges Project has been a dream of the Chinese people for several generations, who have eventually accomplished a relatively feasible scheme through survey, research ,design and demonstration in the past decades. In 1993, the Three Gorges Project entered its implementing stage from the demonstration stage. On December 14, 1994, it was declared to the outside world that the construction of Three Gorges Project was officially started.

The Three Gorges Project mainly consists of such main structures as river dam, flood discharge dam, hydropower stations, double-line five-stage continuous ship lock, ship lifts and upstream/downstream navigation channels. From construction preparation in 1993 to overall completion in 2009, the Three Gorges Project features a total construction period of 17 with the construction implemented in three phases. Phase I Project commenced in 1993 and ended in 1997, marked by the river closure; Phase II Project commenced in 1998 and ended in 2003, marked by initial water impoudment in the reservoir, operation of the double-line five-stage ship lock and commissioning of the first generating units; Phase III Project commenced in 2004 and will be completed in 2009, marked by commissioning of all generating units and completion of the entire water control project.

Completion of the Three Gorges Project will bring benefits in ten aspects of flood control, power generation, navigation, aquiculture, tourism, ecological protection, environmental purification, development-oriented resettlement, south-north water transfer and irrigation, outperforming any other large hydropower stations in the world.

Bird's-Eye View of the Dam

■ Three Gorges Project on the Yangtze River

Great Events in Three Gorges Project Construction

1. In his "National Construction Strategy II— Industrial Program" early in 1919, Sun Yat-sen, the forerunner of China's Democratic Revolution, initiated the conception to improve the waterway for Chuanjiang River and make use of the Three Gorges for hydropower generation.

2. In October 1932, Chinese Government Resources Committee organized a survey team for hydropower generation on the upper reaches of the Yangtze River. This team conducted a two-month onsite survey and measurement in the Three Gorges region for the first time and compiled "Survey Report for Hydropower Generation on the Upper Reaches of the Yangtze River" in 1933.

3. In May 1944, Dr. Savage, famous dam expert in the world and chief designer and engineer of U.S. Bureau of Reclamation, came to China in response to invitation and conducted onsite survey on the Three Gorges under the shellfire of Japanese invaders. Later, he compiled "Initial Report for Three Gorges Program", the first specific plan to consider comprehensive utilization of waterpower resources in the Three Gorges.

4. October 1949 witnessed the foundation of the People's Republic of China. In February 1950, Yangtze Resources Commission was established in Wuhan. The commission renamed as Yangtze Valley Planning Office from 1956 to 1989.

5. In July 1956, Mao Zedong, the chairman of Chinese government, composed his famous poetry "Cut off the river at Wushan to create a mirror-like lake and create a wonder surprising to the world without affecting the Goddess Peak!", which for the first time portray the grand blueprint for the Three Gorges Project.

6. On March 1, 1958, Zhou Enlai, premier of the State Council, led a team of more than 100 people, including leaders of relevant ministries and commissions, leaders of provinces and municipalities along the Yangtze River as well as Chinese and Soviet experts for a survey on the Nanjinguan and Sandouping Dam sites in the Three Gorges. Premier Zhou Enlai specifically pointed out the preferred dam site for the Three Gorges Project was Sandouping, which represents a critical decision for the site selection of the dam.

7. On March 30, 1958, Mao Zedong went on an inspection tour by Jiangxia Yacht to the Three Gorges before attending CPC Central Committee Chengdu Conference.

8. On April 25, 1958, CPC Central Committee Chengdu Conference adopted the "Views of the CPC Central Committee on Three Gorges Water Control Project and Yangtze River Valley Planning", the first document of the CPC Central Committee concerning the Three Gorges Project.

9. On December 26, 1970, the Central Committee and State Council approved the construction of the Gezhouba Water Control Project as a part of the Three Gorges Water Control Project and pointed out that this was a preparatory project for planned and phased construction of the Three Gorges Project. Gezhouba Project started power generation in 1981 and was fully completed in 1989.

10. In February 1984, the State Council approved in principle the "Feasibility Study Report of the Three Gorges Water Control Project" formulated by the Yangtze Valley Planning Office, initially defined low-dam scheme of 150m water storage level for the Three Gorges Project, and decided to establish Preparatory Leading Group for Three Gorges Project Construction, Preparatory Group for and China Three Gorges Project Corporation.

11. In late 1984, Chongqing CPC Committee submitted "View and Comments Regarding the Three Gorges Project" to the Central Committee, in which, Chongqing CPC Committee specifically objected to the 150m scheme for the Three Gorges Project and proposed a 180m scheme. Objecting to the low-dam scheme also includes CPPCC (Chinese People's Political Consultative Conference) members and social groups.

12. In June 1986, the Central Committee issued "Circular of the CPC Central Committee and State Council on the Issues Regarding the Demonstration of the Three Gorges Project" and instructed the Ministry of Water Conservancy and Electric Power to organize experts in various disciplines to seek comments, further demonstrate and revise the original Feasibility Study Report of the Three Gorges Project, and propose another Feasibility Study Report, and subsequently dissolved Preparatory Group for Three Gorges Province. Based on the decision of the Central Committee, the Ministry of Water Conservancy and Electric Power established 14 expert groups which spent 3 years in full demonstration.

13. On March 6, 1992, Premier Li Peng submitted "Proposal of the State Council Regarding the Construction of the Three Gorges Project" to the Fifth Conference of the Seventh Plenary Session of National People's Congress (NPC). On April 3, 1992, 2633 NPC deputies voted on the proposal, including 1767 affirmative votes, 177 negative votes, 644 waivers and 25 invalid votes and this proposal was finally adopted. Afterwards, the Three Gorges Project went through demonstration and entered its implementing stage. As a result, the century-long dream of the Chinese people eventually came true.

Full view of the five-step shiplock

The vertical shiplift

Power plant on left bank

Power plant on right bank

Flood Discharge Dam Section

Yangtze River

Layout of the Three Gorges Project

Three Gorges Project on the Yangtze River

Zhongbaodao-Insel inn Original

Dam Site of Three Gorges Project

Dam Site and normal water level are basic and critical factors to determine the scale, benefit and construction difficulty for a water control project as well as the solution of a series technical issues.

The Three Gorges Dam is located on Zhongbao Island at Sandouping Town in Yichang, Hubei. It has taken more than several decades to select the dam site for the Three Gorges Propect. When selecting dam site in the 1950s, comparison was made for 15 sites at two dam areas and Sandouping was initially selected as the site. In consideration of such factors as engineering protection and phased development, comparison was made for two sites, Shibei and Taipingxi, in early 1960s. Eventually, Zhongbao Island at Sandouping was selected as the dam site for Three Gorges Project in the 1980s.

Geologically, Sandouping features rigid impermeable granite, and serves as ideal foundation for the construction of the high dam. In addition, Sandouping features wide river valley and shallow hills on both banks, which is easy to be expanded and convenient for construction. Longitudinal cofferdam can be constructed on Zhongbao Island in the center of the river, dividing the Yangtze River into 900m-wide major river and 300m-wide river, which creates favorable landform conditions for phased diversion construction of the riverbed.

Rock Core Drilled at Dam Site

■ Three Gorges Project on the Yangtze River

三峡工程
CHINA
中国 Three Gorges Project

Construction Scheme for
the Three Gorges Project

Planning of Construction Period

The TGP construction is divided into three phases according to the river diversion procedures.

The construction of a water project is undertaken on the dry ground,so the river has to be closed to form a construction pit,water in the pit is pumped dry, and weathered rocks at the dam foundation are removed completely to build the dam on fresh rocks. That is why a river has to be closed and diverted in the construction so as to allow water through other courses downstream.

Zhongbaodao Islet,situated in the middle of the river,divideds the Yangtze River into the major and rear rivers,and provides a favourable terrain for the construction of phased river diversion.

Project Construction :TGP is constructed by using the scheme of one cascade development, completion at one-time impoundment by stages and continuous resettlement .The project is constructed in three phase with a total construction period of 17 years.

Phase 1 construction :

1993 to 1997,The rear river was closed by rock and earth cofferdams to construct an open diversion channel. The river water flowed and ships sailed through the main river channel of the Yangtze River.The closure of the major river of the Yangtze River in 1997 marked the completion of the first-phase construction and the start of the second-phase construction.

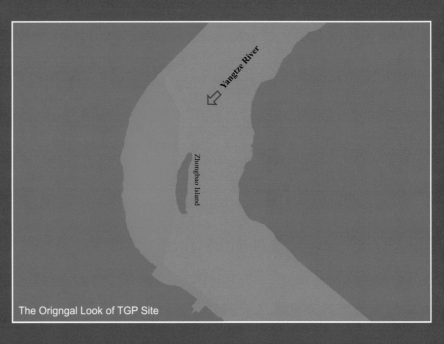

The Origngal Look of TGP Site

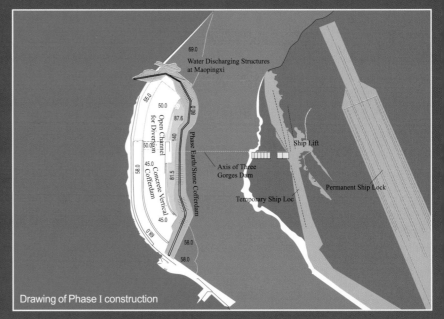

Drawing of Phase I construction

Phase 2 Construction:

1998 to 2003,The main targets were to build the spillway dam section,the left-bank dam section and the left-bank powerhouse with the phase II foundation pit.The river flowed through the open diversion channel and ships sailed through the diversion channel or the temporary ship lock.The closure of the open diversion channel marked the end of the second phase construction.

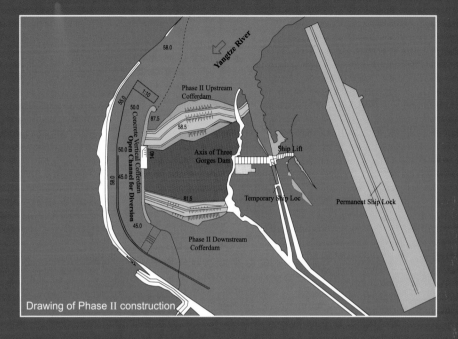

Drawing of Phase II construction

Phase 3 Construction:

2004 to 2009,The third-phase construction pit was formed by building upstream RCC cofferdam and down-stream rock-and-earth cofferdam to construct the right-bank dam section and the powerhouse.The river dis-charges through 23 deep outlets and 22 temporary bot-tom outlets in the spillway and ships sail through the dual-line and five-step ship lock. The overall completion of the hydraulic structures and commissioning of all generating units marks the end of the third-phase construction.

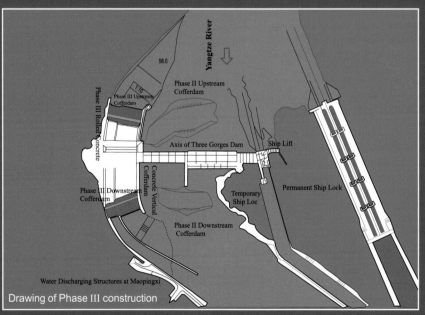

Drawing of Phase III construction

Three Gorges Project on the Yangtze River

Construction Site of Dam on Right Bank

Three Gorges Project on the Yangtze River

三峡工程
CHINA
中国 Three Gorges Project

Construction Scheme for
the Three Gorges Project

Panoramic View of Phase III Construction Site

■ Three Gorges Project on the Yangtze River

三峡工程
CHINA
中国 Three Gorges Project

Construction Scheme for
the Three Gorges Project

Hoisting of Foundation Loops

Night Scene of Phase III Construction Site

Three Gorges Project on the Yangtze River

River Diversion and Closure

Based on extensive research of experts and constructors in the past years, the construction of the Three Gorges Project is implemented by a phased diversion scheme, namely "Thrice cofferdams, twice closure, three-phase diversion, open diversion channel , and ship lock for navigation during construction".

The key task of the first step was to construct longitudinal concrete cofferdams on Zhongbaodao Island, retain water with earth-rock cofferdams and cut open diversion channel in compliance with the requirements of diversion, construction and navigation while constructing the foundation for the Phase III concrete cofferdams. During this period, the main river channel was still used for flood discharge and navigation. The second step was to close on the main river channel for the first time, retain water with upstream and downstream cofferdams and construct foundation pit for Phase II construction on the main river channel and the bench land on the left bank to facilitate Phase II construction. In this period, completed open diversion channel was used for diversion and navigation

and the completed temporary ship lock on the left bank is used for navigation, which substantially reduced construction cycle. The third step was to implement the second river on the open diversion channel after the completion of Phase II construction, and construct RCC cofferdams in the low-water season to form foundation pit to facilitate Phase III construction. In this period, the diversion bottom outlets constructed in the discharge dam body was used for water discharge. After the second closure is completed and before the initial water storage level at Three Gorges Reservoir reached up to EL.135m, the temporary ship lock became nullified. As a result, "Cross-dam transport" measures were taken to transport cross-dam personnel and materials by land. After about half a year when the water storage level reached 135m, a dual-channel and five-step permanent ship lock for the Three Gorges Project was put into operation on June 16, 2003. As shown in practice, this scheme is quite a success.

Clousure of the Yangtze River (November 1997)

Open Diversion Channel Clousure (November 2002)

Successful Cutoff of Open Channel for Diversion(November 2002)

Three Gorges Project on the Yangtze River

三峡工程

CHINA

Three Gorges Project

Construction Scheme for the Three Gorges Project

Open Diversion Canal in Navigation

Cross-Dam Transportation

External Transportation for the Construction of the Three Gorges Project

During the construction period of the Three Gorges Project, large quantities of materials and equipments particularly large or heavy-duty equipment have to be transported in the cite. Through research and demonstration by experts, a cost-effective solution of "Road Transport Assisted by River Transport" is adopted for transportation of the project. Road transportation is via the expressway from Yichang to the dam area, connecting Yichang-Wuhan Expressway in the east. As shown in practice , this is a right solution.

Xiling Yangtze Bridge

Expressway Special for Three Gorges Project

The Liantuo Bridge

■ Three Gorges Project on the Yangtze River

Flood Discharge Dam Section for the Three Gorges Project

Located at the central part of the dam (i.e., the main river channel of the Yangtze River), the flood discharge dam section of the Three Gorges Dam is 483m in full length. Connected with left and right hydropower stations, the flood discharge dam section has twenty-three 7m-wide, 9m-high deep outlets and twenty-two surface outlets with 8m clear width as well as water discharge outlets with other functions, featuring 102,500m3/s in maximum discharge capacity (excluding generating units).

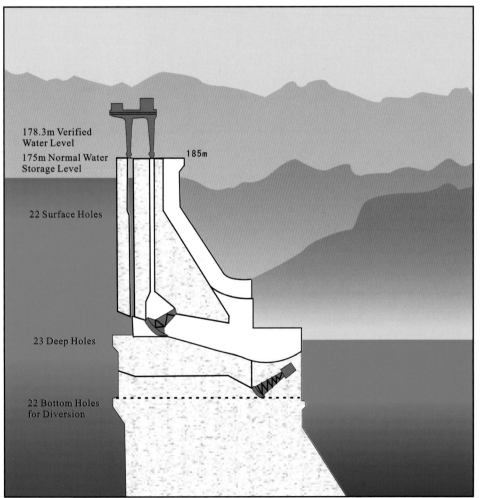

178.3m Verified Water Level

175m Normal Water Storage Level

185m

22 Surface Holes

23 Deep Holes

22 Bottom Holes for Diversion

Schematic drawing for Flood Discharge Dam Section

Flood Discharge Dam Section

Three Gorges Project on the Yangtze River

三峡工程

Flood Discharge Dam section

Flood Discharge Dam Section

Crest of Flood Discharge Dam Section

Three Gorges Project on the Yangtze River

Navigation Buildings for the Three Gorges Project

Navigation buildings for the Three Gorges Project include dual-channel and five-step permanent ship locks and ship lifts arranged in the mountains on the left bank of the dam. The ship lock is 6442m in full length and its main body section is 1607m in length. The upstream and downstream approach channel are 2113m long and 2722m long respectively. The effective size of a single step lock chamber for the dual-channel and five-step ship lock is 280 x 34 x 5m (Long x Wide x Minimum water depth), enabling 50 million t one-way annual throughput and passing 10,000t fleets.

The dual-channel and five-step ship lock is excavated and constructed in the granite mountain, known as the "Fourth Gorge" on the Yangtze River. To ensure the stability of high slopes and restrict its deformation, high slopes are supported in time by anchor bars and shotcrete during construction period, in addition, more than 3600 300t-grade prestressed tendons and over 100,000 high-strength anchor bars are provided at the slopes. On June 15, 2003, the dual-channel and five-step ship lock of the Three Gorges Project was successfully put into trial navigation.

The double-lane sive-stepshiplock service

Virgin Navigation

■ Three Gorges Project on the Yangtze River

Panorama of the double-lane five-step shiplock

Three Gorges Project on the Yangtze River

三峡工程 ■

CHINA

Three Gorges Project

Navigation Buildings

Temporary Ship
Lock

The ship lift

The ship lift is a single-line and one-step vertical lift where the effective size of the ship chamber is 120 x 18 x 3.5m. The ship lift can lift a 3,000t-10 ship at a time, taking about 45 minutes to cross the dam.

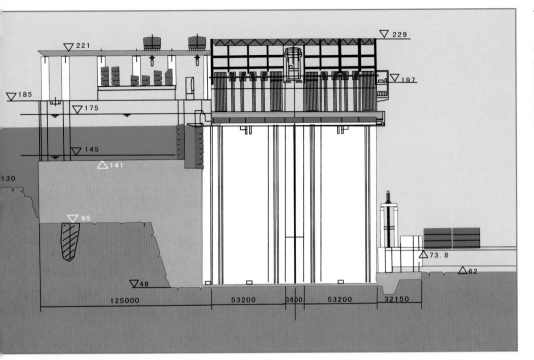

The greatest difference between the Three Gorges Dam and other dams in the world is that the world's largest ship lock and ship lift will be built on it . Ship lock and ship lift work in principle similar to elevator. When taking elevators, you may have to wait for some time but elevators will go up at higher speed and take you to a higher destination.

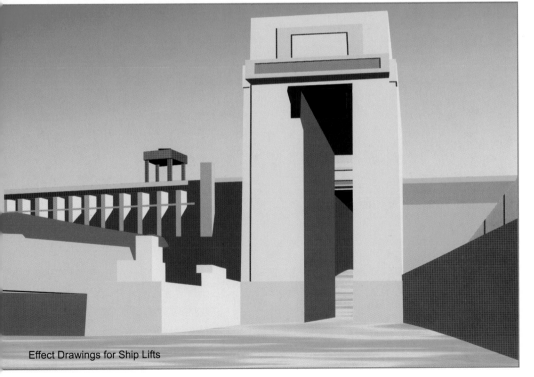

Effect Drawings for Ship Lifts

Power Stations for the Three Gorges Project

Power stations for the Three Gorges Project are left and right bank hydrodectric stations at dam · toe .26 hydropower generating units are installed in total, including 14 in the left powerhouse and 12 in the right powerhouse, with 700MW in single-unit installed capacity as the largest hydropower generating units in the world. In June 2003, the first generating units were integrated with power net and started power generation.

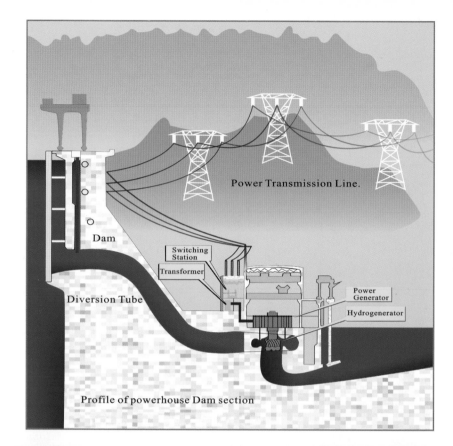

Power Transmission Line.

Dam

Switching Station

Transformer

Power Generator

Hydrogenerator

Diversion Tube

Profile of powerhouse Dam section

1.Left powerhouse for the Three Gorges Project
2.Internal View of the powerhouse
3.Night Scene of the powerhouse

三 峡 水 利 枢 纽 左 岸 电 站 14 台 机 组 全 部 投 产 发 电 仪 式

2

3

■ Three Gorges Project on the Yangtze River

三峡工程 ■

CHINA

Three Gorges Project

Power Station for the Three Gorges Project

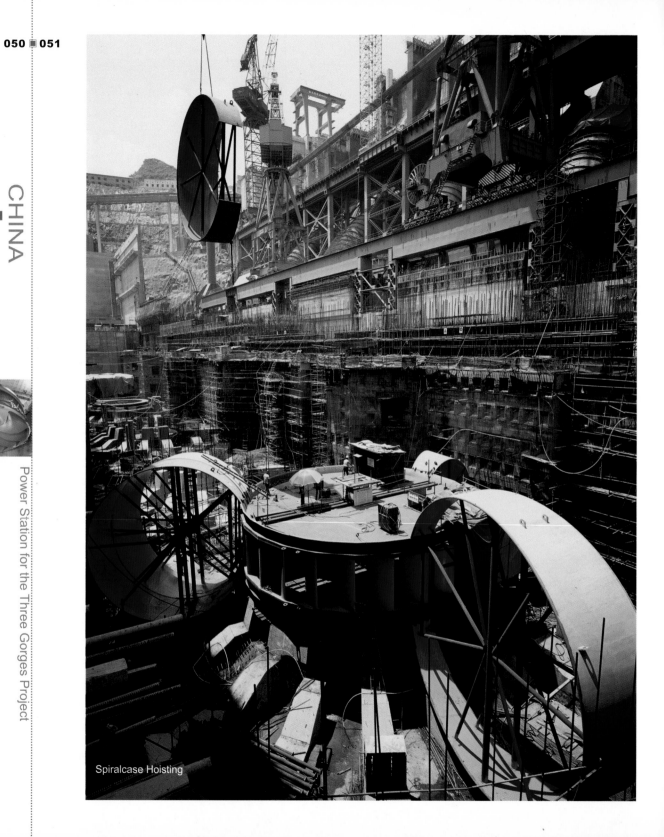

Spiralcase Hoisting

Spiralcase Welding

Spiralcase Construction

三峡工程

Three Gorges Project

Power Station for the Three Gorges Project

The generator rotor of 1,694.5 tons

The greatest turbine runner in the world

东方电机

Three Gorges Project on the Yangtze River

三峡工程

CHINA

Three Gorges Project

Power Station for the Three Gorges Project

Underground powerhouse

Panoramic View of Underground powerhouse

Outlet of Underground powerhouse

三峡工程

CHINA
中国 Three Gorges Project

World Records Created by the Construction of TGP

1.The most remarkable project with flood control benefit in the world

The TGP reservoir, with a total storage capacity of 39.3 billion m^3, 22.15 billion m^3 being flood control capacity, can effectively control floods from the upper reaches of the Yangtze River, therefore, increase the flood control capacity of the middle and lower reaches of the Yangtze River.

2.The largest hydropower plant

The total installed capacity of the Three Gorges Hydropower Plant is 18, 200 MW with design annual output of 84.68 TWh .

3.The largest construction scale

The total length of the dam is 2,309.47 m at its axis. The spillway dam section is 483 m long .Twenty-six hydro turbine-generating units, each with a installed capacity of 700 MW, are installed in the two hydropower plants.The navigation buildings consist of a dual-channel and five-step ship lock and a ship lift 265,500t metal structures are installed in the main structures of the project preparation and imstallation of bars amount to 463,000t, the earth-rock excavation and back filling is 134 million m^3,and the concrete placement is 27. 94 million m^3

4.The maximum concrete placement intensity

The concrete placement of TGP created world records in three successive years, In 2000, the total amount fulfilled amounted to 5.4817 x $10^6 m^3$,with a monthly maximum of 550,000 m^3.

5.The most difficult river diversion

The maximum design discharge for the main river closure was 10,000m^3/s and the height of the cofferdam is 60 m.

6.Spillway with the largest flood discharge capacity

The maximum flood discharge capacity of the spillway is 102,500 m^3/s.

7.River lock with the most steeps and highest water head

The total water head of twin five-stage TGP ship lock is 113 m.

8.The largest and most difficult ship lift

Maximum lifting height of the TGP,s ship Lift is 113m. Its ship chamber has an effective size of 120m x 18m x 3.5m with a total weight of 12,800 tons including water within it. It is capable of passing 3000-ton ships.

The subsidiary dam of the TGP-The Maopingxi dam

Three Gorges Project on the Yangtze River

Comparison of the World's 8 Greatest Hydropower Stations

Country	Hydropower Stations	River	Total installed capacity (MW)	Power generation/year (TWh)
China	Three Gorges	Yangtze River	18200	84.68
Brazil and Paraguay	Itaipu	Parana River	12600	71
USA	Grand Coulee	Colunbia River	10830	20.3 (in the initial stage)
Venezuela	Guri	Caroni River	10300	51
Brazil	Tucurui	Tocantins River	8000	32.4 (in the initial stage)
Canada	La Grande Stage II	La Grande River	7326	35.8
Russia	Sayano-Shushensk	Yenesei River	6400	23.7
Russia	Krasnoyarsk	Yenesei River	6000	20.4

List of Main Features of the Project

Ltem Description		Unit	Index	Note
Reservoir	Normal Pool Level	m	175	156m in the intial stage
	Flood Control Level	m	145	135m in the intial stage
	Design Flood Level	m	175	
	Check Flood Level	m	180.4	
	Total Storage Capacity	Billion m³	39.3	
	Flood Control Capacity	Billion m³	22.15	
	Surface Area	km²	1,084	
Dam	Type		Concrete gravity	
	Crest Elevation	m	185	
	Max.Height	m	181	
	Length of the Axis	m	2,039.47	
Power Station	Length of Left Powerhouse	m	643.7	
	Number of Units in Left Powerhouse	Set	14	
	Length of Right Powerhouse	m	584.2	
	Number of Units in Right Bank	Set	12	
	Capacity per Unit	MW	700	
	Total Installed Capacity (Excluding Underground Powerhouse)	MW	18,200	
	Annual Electricity Output (Excluding Underground Powerhouse)	Twh	84.68	
	Number of Units in Underground powerhouse	Set	6	
	Installed Capacity in Underground powerhouse	MW	4,200	
Ship Lock	Type			Double way,5 stage
	Size of Chamber	m	280×34×5	
Ship Lift	Type			One way,5 stage
	Size of Chamber	m	120×18×3.5	

Three Gorges Project on the Yangtze River

Flood Control

Rainfall in The Yangtze River Basin features monsoon climate and the discharge in flood season from June to September each year accounts for 70-75% in annual total discharge. According to historic records, 214 flood disasters took place in the Yangtze River during the 2096 years from 185 B.C. to 1911 A.D. , once every 10 years on average; and 11 lager flood damages occurred since 1921, once every 6 years on average. As the Mother River for the Chinese Nation, the Yangtze River fostered the Chinese nation and brought about countless disasters for surrounding residents as well. Ancient flood fighting myths and detailed historic literatures have recorded the long history of joy and grief for the Chinese nation in the past 5000 years:

In 1870, an extraordinary flood rare in history took place, setting the land of 160,000km2 in water and causing substantial casualties; in 1931, as many as 145,000 residents fell victim to flood; in 1935, as many as 142,000 residents died of flood; in 1954, flood caused 33,000 deaths; in 1998, flood caused 1,526 deaths;

The key purpose of the Three Gorges Project is flood control.

The dam is designed based on an once-in-1000-year flood standard and checked based on once-in-10000-year plus 10% flood standard, making it a water control project with most significant flood control benefit in today's world. The maximum flood discharge capacity of the Three Gorges Project can reach up to 120,600m^3/s. Though the flood control capacity of 22.15 billion cubic meters for the Three Gorges Reservoir is relatively small compared with the annual average runoff of 960 billion m^3 for the Yangtze River, yet it can reduce peak flood through the dam by approximately 30% by means of "reducing peak and delaying storage", thus effectively restraining the Yangtze River from flooding to the middle and lower reaches of the Yangtze River. As a critical backbone project in the flood control system for the middle and lower reaches of the Yangtze River, the Three Gorges Project will protect the 1,530,000 ha fertile farm lands as well as cities and towns on the Jianghan Plain and the Dongting Lake regions, and ensure the normal living and work for 15 million residents there.

Flood discharge

Flood discharge

■ Substantial Social and Social Economic
Benefits from the Three Gorges Project

三峡工程
CHINA
中国 Three Gorges Project　Flood Control

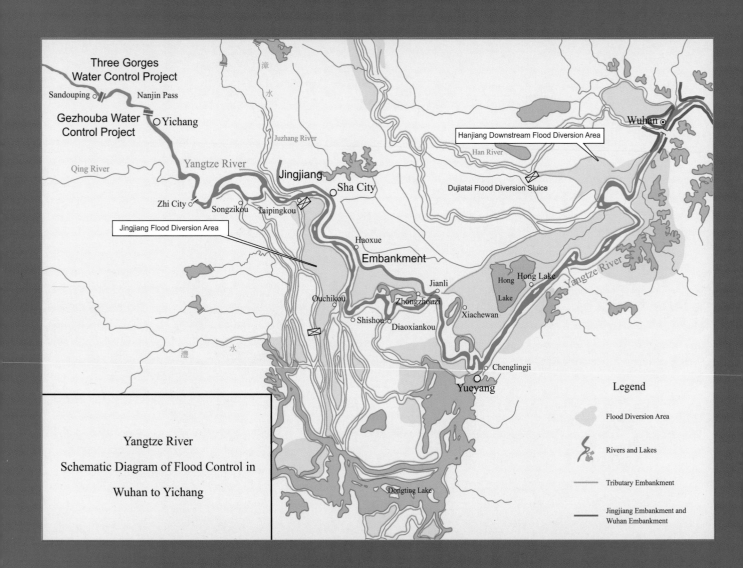

Three Gorges
Water Control Project

Sandouping　Nanjin Pass

Gezhouba Water
Control Project　Yichang

Qing River

Yangtze River

Zhi City

Songzikou

Taipingkou

Jingjiang Flood Diversion Area

Jingjiang

Sha City

漳水

Juzhang River

Hanjiang Downstream Flood Diversion Area

Han River

Dujiatai Flood Diversion Sluice

Wuhan

Haoxue

Embankment

Jianli

Hong Lake

Hong
Lake

Yangtze River

Ouchikou

Zhongzhouzi

Shishou

Diaoxiankou

Xiachewan

澧水

Chenglingji

Yueyang

Dongting Lake

Yangtze River

Schematic Diagram of Flood Control in

Wuhan to Yichang

Legend

Flood Diversion Area

Rivers and Lakes

Tributary Embankment

Jingjiang Embankment and
Wuhan Embankment

Aerial Photo of Jingjiang Flood Control levee

■ Substantial Social and Social Economic
Benefits from the Three Gorges Project

Power Generation

The Yangtze River contains substantial energy sources. As the largest hydropower station in today's world, the Three Gorges Hydropower Station consists of two powerhouses on the left and right banks of the flood discharge dam, 1210m in full length. Left and right powerhouse is equipped with 14 and 12 hydropower generating units, respectively. The Three Gorges Hydropower Station houses 26 hydropower generating units in total with 700MW in rated installed capacity for single unit and 18,200MW in total installed capacity. The average annual power generation is 84.68TWh, equivalent to the power generated by 6 Gezhouba hydropower stations or 10 Dayawan nuclear power stations. The Three Gorges Hydropower Station is the largest hydropower station in today's world in terms of either single unit capacity or total installed capacity.

To bring the economic benefit in power generating of the Three Gorges Project into full play, an underground hydropower station will be built in the mountain on the right bank of the Three Gorges Dam, including 6 hydropower generating units with 700MW in rated installed capacity for single unit and 4,200MW in total installed capacity. The water inlet was constructed simultaneously with the Three Gorges Project. Generating sets in underground hydropower station alone is equivalent to 1.5 Gezhouba hydropower stations. As a result, the Three Gorges Project has 32 hydropower generating units in total with 22,400MW in total installed capacity.

The radius of economic power supply by the Three Gorges Hydropower Station is 1,000km, covering a major part of China's territory and featuring substantial advantages in geographical location. Currently, the hydropower station supplies power to Central China, East Sichuan and South China via 500KV AC distribution line and to East China via 500KV DC distribution line. It will supply reliable, cheap, clean renewable energy sources to economically-advanced yet resources-scarce regions such as East China, Central China and South China.

Central Control Room of Three Gorges Hydropower Station

First HV take-off Tower of on Left Hydropower Station

■ Substantial Social and Social Economic
Benefits from the Three Gorges Project

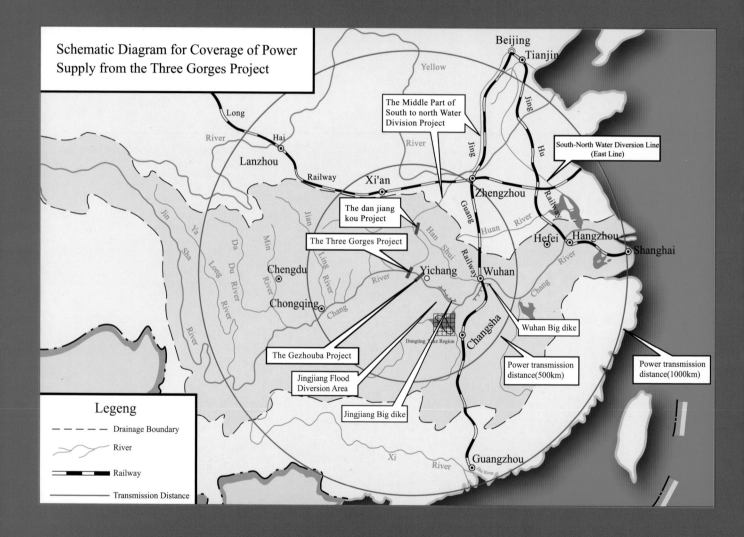

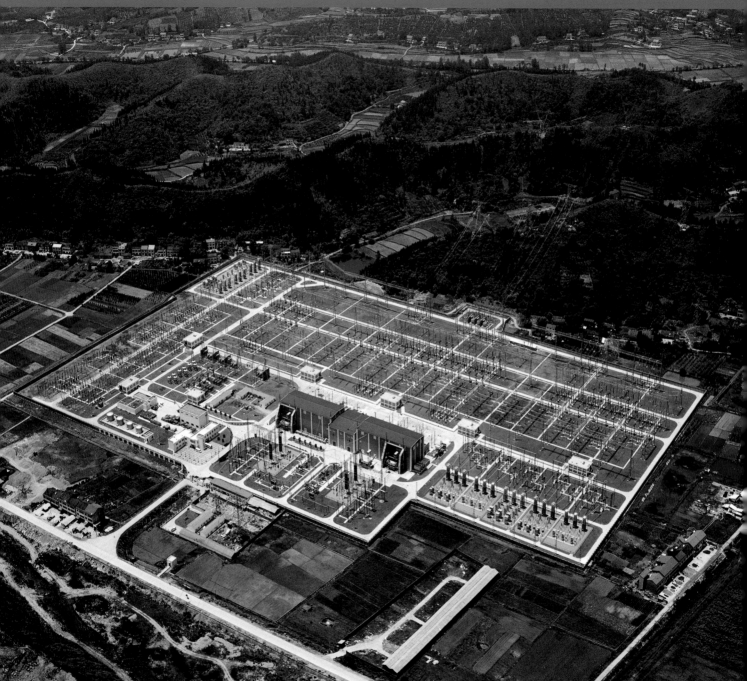

Longquan Converter Station

□ **Substantial Social and Social Economic Benefits from the Three Gorges Project**

Navigation

The Yangtze River has been known as "prime river channel". However, the river channel of the Chuanjiang River (section of the Yangtze River in Sichuan) and navigation reach in Three Gorges features torrential current and too many shoals, hence the ancient saying "Walking on the narrow paths of Sichuan is as difficult as climbing up to the heaven". It can be asserted that the history of navigation in Chuanjiang River is a history of blood and tears. Though many reef-blasting projects were implemented since the foundation of the People's Republic of China, yet the river channel remained obstructed. The river channel is narrow in many sections and only small ships under 1000t can navigate. Also, the Jingjiang River section in the middle reaches of the Yangtze River can only accommodate small ships under 1000t in dry season.

After completion, the Three Gorges Project can create sub-stantial benefit for navigation, turning the river channel of Chuanjiang River into prime river channel in true sense without its previous torrential current and extensive shoals. The 660km river channel from Yichang to Chongqing will be substantially improved and 10,000t ships can directly navigate to Chongqing. As a result, the one-way annual trafficability of the river channel will be increased from 10 million t to 50 million t Due to decelerated flow velocity and improved safety for night navigation, ships can substantially reduce navigation time and reduce transportation cost by 35-37%. This can effectively change the current status of obstructed navigation during dry season in the middle reaches of the Yangtze River, set navigation in the Yangtze River into a new epoch and create farourable conditions for the economic development in Central and West China.

Prime River Channel of the Yangtze River

New waterway in Three Gorges after impoundment

■ Substantial Social and Social Economic
Benefits from the Three Gorges Project

三峽工程

CHINA

Three Gorges Project

Navigation

Signal Tower for Navigation

Prints Left on Rock by Three Gorges Boat Trackers

Precipice Plank Paths in Xiajiang

Three Gorges Boat Trackers

三峡工程
CHINA
中国 Three Gorges Project

One Million Residents
for Resettlement

Resettlement for the Three Gorges Reservoir is deemed as a world-class problem and a critical factor to decide the fate of the Three Gorges Project. The Three Gorges Project is an extraordinary project in the world, rare in the history of water control projects of the world in terms of the number of residents to be resettled and quantities of premises to be submerged. At 175m normal pool level, the reservoir will mundate 21 counties (cities and districts) in Hubei and Chongqing and 28, 000 hectares of tarm land, orchards and forestland. This requires the resettlement of 1.136 million residents, known as "One Million Residents for Resettlement". Based on the price in May 1993, the total static investment for resettlement compensation of the Three Gorges Reservoir region hits RMB 40 billion.

The construction of the Three Gorges Project follows the policy of "one cascade development, completion at one-time, impoundment by stages and continuous resettlement", which creates favorable conditions for governments at different levels to properly implement resident resettlement. By late 2002, 689,400 residents had been resettled, most of whom were resettled around the reservoir region with noticeable improvement in living quality; and about 100,000 residents were resettled outside the reservoir region, distributed in 25 provinces, municipalities and autonomous regions around the country. On the other hand, the implementation of a series of "Development-oriented resettlement" policies enacted by the state laid a solid foundation for resettled residents of the Three Gorges to "Make a better living through resettlement". The success in resettlement of the project is attributable to the solid work of those ordinary Chinese people in the Three Gorges Reservoir region who shoulder this responsibility to ensure proper resettlement and smooth construction of the Three Gorges Project.

Antique Street in Zigui

New County Seat of Wushan

三峽工程

CHINA

Three Gorges Project

One Million Residents for Resettlement

Resettlement of Residents for Three Gorges Project

New County Seat of Ziguis

New Village for Resettlement

Sedimentation

Whether the construction of the Three Gorges Reservoir will cause silt sedimentation or not has attracted extensive concern from various social circles. Therefore, in the design of the Three Gorges Project, extensive attention has been paid to silt sedimentation of the reservoir. Three issues have to be solved: The first is that the reservoir should not lose its effect due to sedimentation; the second is that local sedimentation should not cause navigation obstruction; the third is that the "Storing clear water and sluicing muddy water" measures taken to reduce sedimentation in reservoir should not cause the cutdown of downstream river channel.

To improve sediment discharge of the Three Gorges Reservoir, it is necessary to take proper measures to increase sediment-discharging facilities for the Three Gorges Reservoir in terms of operation dispatching and structures arrangement, and make full use of the favorable conditions of the Three Gorges Project. As a river channel reservoir, the Three Gorges Reservoir is about 600km long in reservoir region and generally less than

1000m wide in reservoir surface (only a small portion is 1000-1700m wide), featuring narrow and deep reservoir surface and few shoals. Sediment flows from the Yangtze River into the reservoir mainly in flood season. As shown by theory and practice in engineering sedimentation both at home amd abroad, application of the "Storing clear water and sluicing muddy water" approach may maintain the effective capacity of the reservoir for long. Specifically, the approach is to reduce water storage level to the flood control level of 145m in flood season from June to September each year and make use of the low-elevation large bottom outlets to seluice flood and sediment (i.e., sluicing muddy water); and raise storage level to normal pool level of 175m when silt flowing into the reservoir substantially decreases after flood season (i.e., storing clear water). Flood regulation in flood season and water storage after flood season may also create some sedimentation in effective reservoir capacity, but this sedimentation may be substantially washed away by maintaining low water level in flood season, only leaving a small amount of sediment at shal-

Clear Water Storage in Reservior

low shoals. As time goes on in operation, sediment sluiced to the downstream of the dam in flood season will be increased until balanced sedimentation is achieved. Application of this approach may maintain long-term operation of the Three Gorges Reservoir.

Another way to reduce sediment into the Three Gorges Reservoir is to make efforts to construct soil and water conservation projects and protection forest projects at the upper reaches of the dam and build large reservoirs at tributaries to block off some sediment.

Flushing in Flood Season

Some sediment impounded by Large Reservoir

■ Solutions to Major Issues for the
Three Gorges Project

Ecological and Environment Protection

Implementation of this world-class project has brought about world-class challenges. In consideration of ecological environment protection and long-term development, objective analysis and coverall planning have been implemented concerning environment, resettlement and funds since the beginning of Three Gorges Project planning, and various issues have been properly solved in a scientific manner in an attempt to build the Three Gorges Reservoir region into an ecological economic zone with attractive environment and good water/soil conservation within 20 to 30 years after the completion of the Three Gorges Project.

With the phased implementation of reservoir impoundment, the Three Gorges Dam began to play the role of flood control in 2003. In June, the dual-channel and five-step ship lock was put into navigation. In July, the first generating unit of the Three Gorges Hydropower Stations began to generate power, which marked the beginning of the environmental and economic benefits of the Three Gorges Project. To sum up, the implementation of the project has played an important role in improving the ecological environment and promoting the sustainable development of economy and society in the Yangtze River Basin.

The purpose of constructing the Three Gorges Project is to promote sustainable growth of the ecological environment on the Yangtze River. Research concerning the impact of the Three Gorges Project on environment got started in the 1950s. As concluded through the research, the Three Gorges Project will have great significance in improving the eco system and environment in the Yangtze River.

The Three Gorges Hydropower Station provides substantial amount of clean energy. Each year, it can save 40-50 million t raw coal compared with coal-fired power stations, and reduces discharge of about 100 milliont carbon dioxide, 20 million t sulfur dioxide, 10,000t carbon monoxide and 370,000t nitrogen oxide as well as a substantial amount of flash and waste dregs, thus noticeably reducing such hazards as greenhouse effect and acid rain, and effectively improving environment in East and Central China.

The focus of ecological and environmental protection for the Three Gorges Project is to implement water quality protection project in the reservoir region to improve the water quality in the lower reaches of the Yangtze River. Some river sections in the Three Gorges Reservoir region feature serious water pollution. To solve this problem, a full range of sewage treatment plants have been constructed during the construction of the Three Gorges Project to improve water quality. Through operation regulation in the reservoir to stabilize discharge in the lower reaches of the Yangtze River, this facilitates effluent control in the lower reaches and thus improves the water quality of the river sections in the lower reaches in dry season, reduces the intrusion of salty water at the estuary of the Yangtze River in low water period and improves water quality for Shanghai.

The construction of the Three Gorges Project can also avoid environmental deterioration and occurrence and or spreading of infectious diseases arising from flooding and flood diversion; facilitate industrial development in every aspect in the reservoir region; noticeably improve local climate in the reservoir region and creates favorable conditions for the development of farming, forestry and fishery. The Three Gorges Project will trigger booming growth in every sector, which, in turn, will inject vitality into the Three Gorges Project and gradually shape ecological balance suitable for human living.

After water storage impoundment, the Three Gorges Reservoir will also create reliable water sources for South-to-North Water Transfer Project in China.

Ecological Harmony in Three Gorges Reservoir Region

■ Solutions to Major Issues for the
Three Gorges Project

Geology and Earthquake

The Three Gorges Dam site is located on Zhongbao Island at Sandouping Town in Yichang, Hubei and specifically, it is located on the crystalline rock formed in the Presinian Period. The riverbed features relatively thin superstratum and the bedrock is granite. The thickness of the weathered layer rock on both banks is about 20-30m but the weathered layer at the riverbed is relatively thin with consistent lithology, complete rock mass and high mechanical strength for bedrock. The rock mass mainly features weak permeability, small scale in fracture, steep angles and excellent bonding. Within more than 10km range upstream and downstream where crystalline rock is distributed, neither active fracture nor adverse physical/geological phenomenon exists.

The region where the Three Gorges Project lies does not have the background to produce violent earthquakes. Huangling massif where the dam site lies features high stability, weak seismic intensity, low earthquake frequency and weak shock environment. In a word, it is a region of weak seismic activities.

The phenomenon of reservoir-induced earthquake is a kind of phenomenon for naturally structural earthquake to disperse and release energy in advance when induced by reservoir impoundment. Earthquake is an event that occurs within a very short time. Therefore, the "superimposed" occurrence for reservoir-induced earthquake and natural earthquake is almost impossible. Based on analysis of various adverse conditions, earthquakes that affect the dam, even if they occur, will not exceed Grade 7 on Richter scale in anti-seismic design for engineering structures and therefore, will not affect the safety of the entire Three Gorges Project.

Bed Rock Excavation for Left Dam

Bed Rock for Dam

Solutions to Major Issues for the
Three Gorges Project

Twilight at Dam

Threat from War

The Three Gorges Project is not only vital importance to the energy supply for Central China, East China and Southwest China, but also an important transportation artery extending from east to west in China. Therefore, it will inevitably become an important target for enemy attack in time of war. As a result, in the construction of the Three Gorges Project, it is necessary to consider how to deal with war threat.

The Three Gorges Project is located at the hinterland in our country and the Three Gorges Dam is of concrete gravity dam. Thanks to its geographic location and firm structure, it has strong capacity to resist attack from conventional weapons. In terms of war threat, it is necessary to consider for the worst situation, including the approach to deal with the situation when the Three Gorges Dam breaks due to attack of nuclear weapon by enemy. In addition to constructing indispensable protection facilities as engineering countermeasures, the largest flood discharge sluice in the world for water control projects has been built to meet the requirements of reducing water storage in reservoir in time of war. Every war has an evolutive process before breakout. In time of warning, the Three Gorges Reservoir may decrease water storage in advance to minimize potential hazard to downstream areas in case of dam break. Meanwhile, as shown through research by experts, there is a 30km-long narrow bend downstream of the dam, which may regulate water storage and reduce flood energy when the dam breaks and flood discharges due to attack. In this way, velocity and discharge will be substantially decreased out of Nanjinguan Pass. When the flood from dam break enters hilly areas, flood flow will become smooth and gradually weaken such that the river channel can safely discharge flood. This may minimize potential hazard from the dam break flood to the downstream areas. In extremely urgent situation, we may further lower water level until most water bodies in the reservoir become dry and let the hydropower station become a run-off hydropower station. This may fundamentally reduce and minimize the potential hazard from dam break.

Financing Sources

The massive and long-term TGP construction necessitates diversified financing channels,which mainly consist of capital in cash from China government,loans from the State Development Bank of China (SDB) and domestic commercial banks, corporate bonds, equity financing, and export credits and foreign exchange loans from foreign syndicate.

1.Capital in cash:

Include Three Gorges Project Construction Funds(up price caused by power), Power revenues from Gezhouba Hydropower Plant(Before the restructuring), Reimbursement from income taxes and dividends of China Yangtze Power Company Ltd.(CYPC), Power revenue and reimbursement from income from Three Gorges Power Station. These four sources contribute nearly RMB80 billion yuan to the project, accounting for approximately 45% of the total project investment(RMB180 billion yuan). The Three Gorges Project Construction Funds, invested into the project construction as the state capital in cash, is the most reliable financing source.

2.Policy loans from SDB:

SDB, as a national policy bank, started to provide loans for TGP at the initial construction of the project. SDB provided the loan from 1994 to 2003 with an annual sum of RMB 3 billion yuan, totaling RMB 30 billion yuan which played an active role in the smooth progress of the construction.It is one of the most stable financing sources.

3.Corporate bonds:

Low-cost construction fund was raised directly from the capital market.Up to the end of 2003, six Three Gorges Bonds were issued with total proceeds of RMB19 billion yuan.

4.Equity financing:

CYPC as a new window for CTGPC's equity financing,was successfully listed on capital market in 2003, and broadened the financing channel for TGP construction.

Loans from domestic commercial banks,export credits, foreign exchange loans from foreign syndicates: The remaining loans amounted to RMB11 billion yuan until the end of 2003.

Item Name	Unit	Parameters
Total static investment	RMB Billion yuan	90.09
Hydraulis structures	RMB Billion yuan	50.09
Compensation due to reservoir inundation	RMB Billion yuan	40
Total dynamic investment	RMB Billion yuan	203.9
Estimated total investment	RMB Billion yuan	180

Economic and Financial Analysis of the Project

During the periods of feasibility study and preliminary design, a comprehensive analysis on TGP's economical and financial feasibility and rationality was made in the principle of "responsibility for the future". The conclusion was that it is economically beneficial and financially viable to construct the Three Gorges Project.As stated in "Report on the Preliminary Design of Three Gorges Project (issued in December 2003)", the internal rate of return is 11.25%, the payback period of loans is 24.59 years, and the payback period of investment is 19. 2 years.

In 2003, CTGPC successfully achieved the three major goals of TGP construction, namely initial impoundment of the reservoir, operation of the ship lock, and commissioning of the first generating units. And then it smoothly entered into the phase III construction. In view of the execution of the investment plans so far, it is predicted that the total investment can be controlled within RMB 180 billion, and the economic benefit of the project will be higher than that assessed during the feasibility study and preliminary design periods.

Aerial Photo of Three Gorges Project

三峡工程
CHINA
中国 Three Gorges Project

Gezhouba Water Control Project as a part of the Three Gorges Project

The Gezhouba Dam is the first key water conservancy project across the Yangtze River. It is a large-scale hydropower station, which was researched, designed and built by our own country. Located in the urban area of Yichang city at the exit of the Yangtze Three Gorges, the Gezhouba Dam is 2.3 kilometers far from Nanjin Pass at the mouth of the Xiling Gorge, and 38 kilometers far from the Three Gorges Dam in the upper position. After rushing out of Nanjin Pass, the Yangtze River suddenly becomes open and wide. Its width expands from 300 to over 2200 meters, The river was separated into three currents by two islands, Gezhouba and Xiba, The hydropower project was named for being built here.

The Gezhouba Hydropower project is 2605.5 meters long and 70 meters high. Covering about 9 square kilometers, the station includes the dam across the river, 3 ship locks, 2 hydropower generation houses, a water spill lock and 2 sand wash locks and a water block wall. The 27-bay flood discharge lock can discharge a water volume of 110 tjpisamd cibic meters per second. All 21 sets of generators with a total installed capacity about 2.715 million kW can generate alectricity 15.7 billion kWh annually. The electricity is transported to Shanghai, Henan, Hunan, Wuhan and other big cities, There are three single-stage locks, of which , two can allow the passage of 10000-ton jumbo ships. The total annual single-way transportation capacity of the ship locks is over 50 million tons.

The project started on December 30,1970. The first phase started to reserve water in May 1981. It was completed on December 20, 1998. The total investment of the project cost RMB4.8 billion yuan. Standing the test of the two historical heaviest floods happened in 1981 and 1998, the dam stayed safe and sound.

Gezhouba Key Water Conservancy Project

Gezhouba Water Control Project

List of Principle Indices of the Gezhouba Project

Item Description	Unit	Index
Drainage Area	Km²	100×10^4
Designed Pool Level	m	66
Crest Elevation	m	70
Total Storage Capacity	m³	15.8×10^8
Annual Average Runoff	m³/s	14,300
Designed Flood Runoff(Flood in 1788)	m³/s	86,000
Check Flood Runoff(Flood in 1870)	m³/s	110,000
Handled Ship Tonnage of No.2	t	$(1.2\text{-}1.6) \times 10^4$
Handled Ship Tonnage of No.3	t	0.3×10^4
Total Installed output Capacity	kw	271.5×10^4
Annual Average Power Generation	Kwh	160×10^8
Max.Flood Sluice of 27 Outlets	m³/s	86,900
Length of the Axis	m	2,606.5
Concrete Placement	m	1.113×10^4
Earth & rock Excavation and Embankment	m	1.113×10^8
Mental Works	t	7.75×10^4

Gezhouba Dam Ship Lock

Gezhouba Dam Flood Discharging

□ Gezhouba Water Control Project

Preservation of Cultural Relics for Three Gorges

Protection of such historic relics in the Three Gorges Reservoir region as ancient architecture, ancient towns and stone carvings after impoundment has attracted great attention from various social circles at home and abroad. "protecting them stay where they are or rebuildngs them elsewhere" measures are taken as planned to protect these historic relics to be submerged or affected, such as White Crane Ridge, Zhang Fei Temple, Shibaozhai Fortress and Qu Yuan Temple. General survey has been conducted to unearth and protect ancient tombs under submerged area.

Shibaozhai Fortress in Zhongxian County

Located in Zhongxian County, Chongqing on the north bank of the Yangtze River, Shibaozhai Fortress was initially built during Kangxi Period (1662~1722AD) in the Qing Dynasty with a history of more than 300 years up to now. The tower consists of 12 stories with 56 in full height, built on a huge boulder rising from a precipice. This boulder is also known as "Jade Seal Mountain". As the legend goes, this is a colorful evil-suppressing stone dropped to the earth when Goddess Nuwa patched the heaven. In later years of Ming Dynasty, Tan Hong rose up in rebellion and occupied this as his fortress, hence the name "Shibaozhai Fortress". Shibaozhai Fortress is a bright pearl in China's ancient architectural art, a national key preservation unit and national "AAAA" tourist spot, listed as one of the eight wonderful buildings in the world.

After water storage level reaches 175m in the Three Gorges Reservoir, Jade Seal Mountain on which Shibaozhai Fortress lies may soften and collapse because mudstone is submerged in water, thus causing deformation to Jade Seal Mountain and affecting the safety for ancient architectures there. Therefore, the key solution for Shibaozhai Fortress protection work is to properly protect ancient cultural buildings, reinforce the massif of Jade Seal Mountain, and ensure proper treatment to underground water and environmental landscape. The new solution adopted now is the "Slope Protection and Steel Reinforcement for Sluice" plan proposed by Changjiang Survey, Planning, research, Design Institute in 2002 with estimated investment exceeding RMB 100 million yuan.

On their way by ship via Shibaozhai Fortress in Zhongxian County, Chongqing after completion of the Three Gorges Project, tourists can see the only island in the Three Gorges Reservoir region. Hosting Shibaozhai Fortress, this island will become the world's largest "Bonsai" embedded in the misty Yangtze River.

Zhang Fei Temple in Yunyang County

Located at the foot of Feifeng Mountain on the southern bank of the Yangtze River in Yunyang County, Chongqing and separated from Yunyang New County Seat by river, Zhang Fei Temple is constructed in memory of Zhang Fei, a famous Shuhan general in the Three Kingdom period. Zhang Fei Temple consists of a series of unique ancient buildings, looking grand and majestic. Specifically, it consists of 7 main buildings, including Front Temple, Side Temple, Sworn Brothers Building, Cloud Viewing Pavilion, Zhufeng Pavilion, Peony and Deyue Pavilions. The first 5 buildings were constructed in memory of Zhang Fei and the last two buildings were constructed in memory of Du Fu, a famous poet in the Tang Dynasty, who lived there for two years as a visitor. Indeed, Zhang Fei Temple is a rare civil and military temple.

In June 2003, Zhang Fei Temple was relocated in a place near Yangtze River more than ten km upperstream from its original site. The "relocation" of Zhang Fei Temple follows the "Rebuilding as it is" principle. The new Zhang Fei Temple maintains every brick and tile of the old Zhang Fei Temple and in addition, the new site is similar to the old site in an attempt to maintain the original style. Also, the new temple has some additional space for cultural relic display. As a result, the overall effect is substantially improved.

1.Zhufengge,a two-storied pavilion
2.Inside Zhang Fei Temple
3.Zhang Fei Temple in Yunyang

Zhang Fei Temple be-
fore Relocation

Zhang Fei Temple after
Relocation

■ Preservation of Cultural Relics
around Three Gorges

Baidi Town(White King Town)

Baidi Town is situated on the top of Baidi Mountain on the north bank of the west mouth of the Qutang Gorge, one of Three Gorges. The buidings with red walls and green tiles are halfhidden in green and luxuriant trees.It is famous for a poem written by the great poet Li Bai in the Tang Dynasty, "Bidding farewell to Baidi enveloped in colorful clouds , a thousand li return journty is covered in one day. As the monkeys cry ceaselessly on both banks, the light boats speeds padt ten thousand peaks." So, it is a famous scenic spot in the Three Gorges.

According historical records, in the late period of the Western Han Dynasty, Gongsun Shu proclaimed himself the king of Shu kingtom, the Present Sichuan. A well in the town allegedly gave off white steam, shaped like a white dragon, Gongsun Shu declarded himself White King,and renamed the town as White King Town. After Gongsun Shu died, local people built a temple on the mountain and made a statue of him in it . This temple was called as the White King Temple.

In the temple the Mingling Hall,the Wuhou Shrine and the Star-watching Pavilion and other structures built in the Ming and Qing Dynasties, At both sides of the temple are the East and West Tablet Galleries where 74 stone tablets from various dynasties, are preserved. In the front hall of the White King Temple,there are a group of colorful statues "Liu Bei Entrusting his son ", "One who read Romance of the Three Kingdoms knows the story of "Liu Bei Entrusting his son" which occurred right in Badi Town . In 222AD, Lui Bei led 2,000,000 soldiers to the east in order to revenge for Guan Yu ,but Liu Bei was defeated, because Lu Xun ,a general of the East Wu Kingdom,set fire to the camps of Lui Bei's army. So,Liu retreated to Jianping in Wushan County , Liu Bei was so tired that he fell ill. Before his death , he asked Zhuge Liang, his prime minister, to his bed, and entrusted his eldest son Liu Chan, second son Liu Yong and third son Liu Li to Zhuge Liang to take care of them. This is the so-called story of "Liu Bei entrusting his son", Now,standing in Baidi town, you seem to be wandering in the long river of history.

The water level of 139 m of the reservoir didn't affect Baidi Town at all. Now Baidi Town is surrounded by water on three sides and by mountains on one side, Baidi Town, where the famous historical event of "Liu Bei Entrusting his son".

Baodo Town, where the famous historical event of "Liu Bei Entrusting his son" took place in the Three Kingdoms Period 2000 years ago, now has been a beautiful peninsula. With the raise of water storage level of the Three Gorges Project in 2006, it will become a fairy island like Penglai, Shandong Province.

1.Group Statues "Liu Bei Entrusting His Sons"
2.City Gate of Baidi Town
3.Autumn Scenery at Baidi Town

Qu Yuan Shrine

The Qu Yuan Shrine is located in the ancient Guizhou Town. Though this town with a history of over 2300-year is very small, only with a area of 0.6 m², it is of an unchangeable position in history as the witness of the great changes in the Three Gorges and Yangtze River. Here occurred many important events in the past dynasties, glories or disgraces and prosperous or decline...

The Qu Yuan Shrine was built to memorize Qu Yuan, also named Ping, the earliest patriotic poet in China. Born in 340 B.C. in Lepingli, Zigui County, he once served as a supervisor and imperial household administrator in the ancient Chu State. Later, squeezed by treacherous court officials, he was banished to a place to the south of the Yangtze River. When the army of the Qing State captured the Chu, he was so overcome with indignation and sorrow that he jumped into the Miluo River. His poems and articles including Laments at parting, Nine Lyrical Poems and Nine Sacrificial Songs are well known all over the world. In 1953, Qu Yuan is listed as one of the cultural famous men in the world by UNESCO.

Atfer the water level rose to EL 139 m, the Qu Yuan Shrine, a famous scenic spot of the Three Gorges in Zigui, Hubei, was affected little. The Qu Yuan Shrine was moved from Quyuantuo and rebuilt in 1976 due to the construction of the Gezhouba Dam Project. Because the Three Gorges Project will raise pool level again, it has to be removed east to the Phoenix Mountain of Maoping Town in Zigui County.

Qu Yuan Shrine

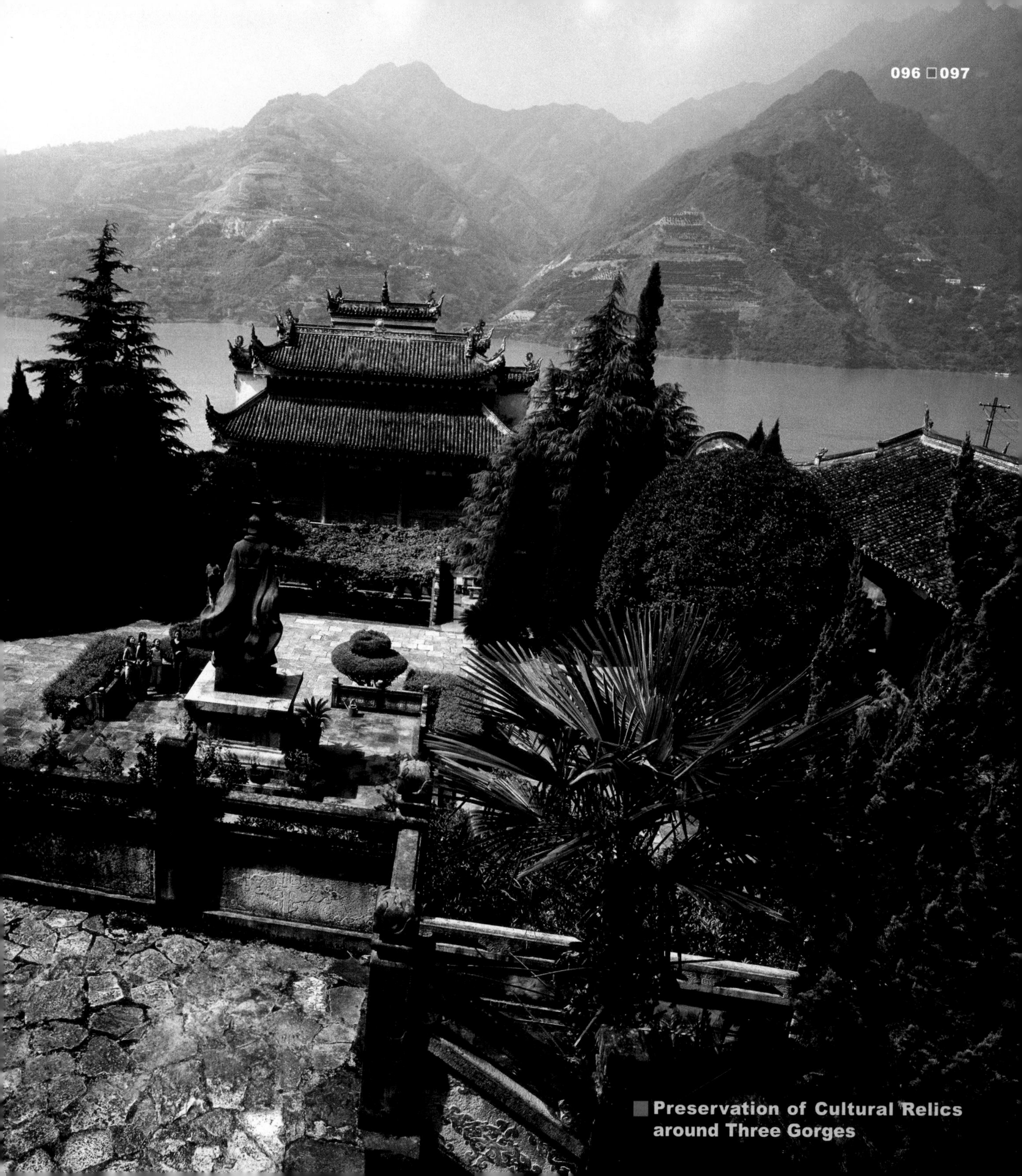

Preservation of Cultural Relics around Three Gorges

Dachang Ancient Town

As the largest town on Daning River, a tributary of Yangtze river in the Three Gorges region, the 1700-year-old Dachang Town in Wushan County is located on the left bank of Daning River, surrounded by water on three sides in the east, west and south. In this ancient town, the east-west main street is 450m long and south-north street is 300m long. The eastern, western and southern city gates remain intact. Houses in town are mostly buildings of the Qing Dynasty, including exquisite carved beams and painted rafters rarely seen in Sichuan Province.

To our relief, with the rise of pool level in 2006,this exquisite ancient town has been fully "cloned" and relocated in a new town a few kilometers away from its original site. The original site of Dachang Ancient Town will become a large lake and the 1700-year-old romance and legend of this ancient town will become our permanent memory.

1.Grotesque Cypresses in the Ancient Town

2.The Southen Gate of the Ancient Town

3.A Corner of Ancient Town

The East Gate of the Ancient Town

Ancient Residential Buildings of Guilin Village in Xintan

The ancient residential buildings of Guilin Village in Xintan are located on the opposite bank of Quyuan Town(the original Xintan Town)in Zigui County in the west section of the Xiling Gorge. They are a group of ancient residential buildings, preserved best, which have the most distinct features and longest history in the whole Three Gorges region.

Before 2002, when every town and county in the Three Gorges still remained,there were only two wowns, which were completely preserved with beautiful mountains and waters and natural residential environment. One is the ancient Dachang Town in Wushan County beside the Daning River, the other is a group of ancient residential buildings built in the Ming and Qing Dynasties of Guilin Village in Xintan Town. In terms of classical degree and artistic standard of the buildings in the two towns as well as local natural sceneries, Guilin village was better than the latter.

The outstanding feature of the ancient residential buildings of Guilin Village, which is different from other local buildings, is called "crooked doors and inclined roads". The doors of these buildings are a little crooked and all the gray-stone alleys seem to stretch slantingly. Experts said that these were caused by the theory of local geomancers, who said that the local geomantic omen was too prosperous,so only "crooked doors and inclined roads" could keep it everlasting. In the Three Gorges , only the ancient Xintan Town on the opposite bank could compare favourably with Guilin Village. Regrettably, it was destroyed in a large landslide in the 1980s. This made Guilin Village come out first. However, after the Three Gorges Project impounds water, Guilin Village has disasppeared completely. Gratifyingly, the main buildings in it have been rebuilt on the phoenix mountain.

Reconstruction of Ancient Buildings

The Phoenix (Fenghuang) Mountain Scenic Spot in Zigui New County Seat is an ancient building reconstruction zone in the Three Gorges Reservoir region.. In memory of Qu Yuan and exhibiting Xiajiang civilization, Qu Yuan Museum is currently built on Phoenix, including Qu Yuan Temple, Tianwen Rostrum, Museum and Chufeng Building. Here, 24 Xiajiang residences and cultural relics are under reconstruction to shape an artistic conception integrating nature, human, history and modern times such that tourists may seem to have entered the cosmic tunnel of history when visiting Xiajiang residences that have been reconstructed or under reconstruction while viewing the Three Gorges Dam from far away. During Dragon Boat Festival each year, Zigui residents in Shuicheng at the foot of Phoenix Mountain still hold boating competition in memory of Qu Yuan, a historic cultural famous man in the world.

Also, Phoenix Mountain is the starting point for New Three Gorges tour after the "Mirror-like Lake" is formed. After water is impounded in the Three Gorges Reservoir, Phoenix Mountain will become a beautiful peninsula. Only 1km from the Three Gorges Dam, Phoenix Mountain features unique geographical location which ignites a kind of enthusiasm and imagination in tourists when viewing the grand and majestic posture of the Three Gorges Dam and the fascinating scenery of the Three Gorges Reservoir.

Jiangdu Temple at Xiling Gorge after Reconstruction

Hydrological Stone Carvings around Three Gorges

On both banks of the Yangtze River are many hydrological inscriptions but most of them are flood inscriptions and very few of them are inscriptions about dry seasons. Of these, the White Crane Ridge Inscription located in the center of the Yangtze River in the north of Fuling City, Chongqing is the most precious inscription with important historic value for scientific research. This 1600m-long, 16m-wide natural stone ridge contains a full rang of stone inscriptions, of which, "Stone fish out of water promises a bumper harvest year" indicates the natural law of bumper harvest years.

After completion and impoundmend of the Three Gorges Project, the White Crane Ridge will remain submerged all the year round. The protection of the White Crane Ridge inscriptions has undergone repeated demonstration and eventually, a protection program has been adopted to protect the original site in "Pressure-free Vessel". The principle of this solution is to construct an underwater protection structure to maintain balance in internal and external water pressure via a filtering device to protect the White Crane Ridge inscriptions. Also, a watertight visitor corridor will be built in the structure connected with ground structure such that visitors can view the White Crane Ridge inscriptions at short distance through load-bearing windows.

After the completion of the Underwater Museum for the White Crane Ridge inscriptions, a huge protection shell will appear on the surface of the reservoir from time to time, attracting countless visitors every day and creating a submarine-like mystery for visitors.

Equally famous as the White Crane Ridge inscriptions in the Three Gorges Reservoir region also include Dragon Bed Stone in Fengdu and Dragon Spine Stone in Yunyang County. With the impoundmend of the Three Gorges Project, these hydrological stone carvings will remain underwater permanently.

1.Dragon Spine Stone
2.Dragon Bed Stone
3.Stone Fish

White Crane Ridge in Fuling

■ Preservation of Cultural Relics
around Three Gorges

Stone Carvings Around Three Gorges

Stone carvings in the Three Gorges region may consist of stele carving, precipice inscription and natural stone carving. These inscriptions are mainly carved on cliff walls on both banks of the river or on shoal reefs and their contents include hydrological inscriptions about flood and dry seasons and binding provisions about the rights and boundary lines of fish farms and forests. Also, this includes event inscriptions about torrential shoal control works, river channel dredging works and charity deeds as well as poetic inscriptions describing fascinating mountains and rivers and personal emotion.

Before impoundment in the Three Gorges Project, measures have been taken to effectively protect precious stone carvings to be submerged. The prestigious precipice carving of the Qutang Gorge has been reconstructed in the "As it is" principle in an attempt to inherit and pass on the history engraved on the precipice.

1."Gap between Hubei and Sichuan" Natural Stone Carving

2.Precipice Stone Carving at Sanyou cave

3.Inscription at Qu Tang Gorge after Reconstruction

Precipice Stone Carving at Qu Tang Gorge after Reconstruction

Tourism of New Three Gorges

As the most fascinating and serene canyon of the Yangtze River and one of the famous scenic spots in China, the Three Gorges is 200km in fully length originating from Baidi Town in Fengjie County, Chongqing in west and ending at Nanjinguan in Yichang, Hubei in east, and consisting of Qutang Gorge, Wuxia Gorge and Xiling Gorge, known as "Three Gorges of the Yangtze River" in full name.

The construction of the Three Gorges Project has stirred up extensive concern: Will the Three Gorges remain fascinating after completion of the project? Precipices on both banks of the Three Gorges are hundreds of meters high and peaks there are as high as 1000-2000m. The water level of the Three Gorges Reservoir will rise by 70-100m compared with natural water level and the water surface of the reservoir will be about 100m wider than natural water surface. Though the visual sense of the gorges will comparatively weaken after reservoir impoundment, yet the Three Gorges will remain her grandeur, uniqueness and serenity. Peaks on both banks of Qutang Gorge are more than 1000m high above sea level, and even when water level rises by more than 40m after completion of the Three Gorges Project, it will only submerge the foot of such peaks and "Kuimen" will remain its posture as the grandest gorge in the world. The Goddess Peak is more than 900m above sea level and submersion of her 50m foot will not greatly affect her attraction. Also, the east section of Xiling Gorge will substantially maintain its original beauty. Mao Zedong portrays this in his famous poetry, "Cut off the river at Wushan to create a mirror-like lake and create a wonder surprising to the world without affecting the Goddess Peak!"

Three Gorges Reservoir impoundment will substantially expand the total area of the Three Gorges Scenic Spot and many scenic spots will have greater value for sightseeing and tourism due to raised water level. Though the visual sense of the Small Three Gorges on the Daning River will be comparatively affected after impoundment, yet the scenic spots around the tributaries of Daning River will increase attraction and serenity. Due to raised water level, Tiny Three Gorges in Madu River will become an attraction. After water level is raised, Shennongxi Stream and Xiangxi River, which originate from the headstream as Daning River, will not only create favorable spots for tourists to experience the river sailing but also form a watercourse for tourists to access the mysterious Shenongjia Scenic Spot and explore the charm of virgin forests. Previously, such scenic spots as Heavenly Geosuture and Gaolan Scenic Spot could be accessed via zigzag mountain paths, but nowadays, they can be accessed by boat.

The Three Gorges Project deserves the title as the most attractive scenery for Tourism New of Three Gorges. When climbing up to the crest of the Three Gorges Dam with grand flood discharge in sight, you may have a strong feeling that no river elsewhere has such extensive cultural contents and no water elsewhere converges so many fascinating spots. When these extensive cultural contents and inspiring waters converge at the Three Gorges Dam, how can they hold back from releasing strong energy? Through this strong energy, we can feel the significance of our ancestors, the significance of our history and the significance of our rivers and mountains!

The construction of the Three Gorges Project not only effectively protects the tourism resources in the Three Gorges region, but also injects new energy and vitality for the development of Three Gorges Tourism, and creates great social and economic benefits. In a word, Three Gorges Tourism gains its rebirth after the construction of the Three Gorges Project!

三峡工程

Goddess Peak

The Clouds and Drizzle Around Wushan Mountain

三峡工程

CHINA

Three Gorges Project

Tourism of New Three Gorges

Spring at Three Gorges

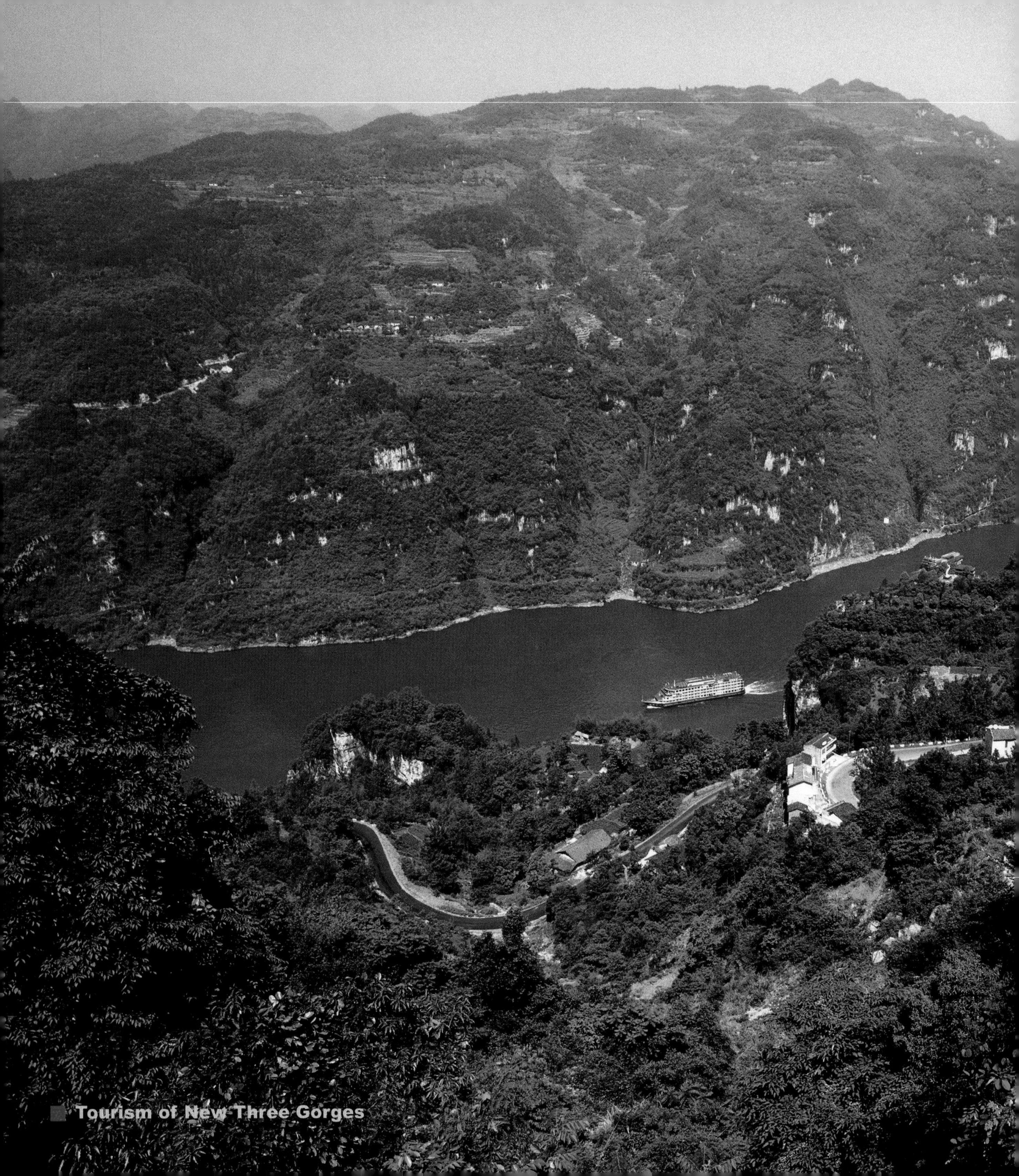

Summer at Three Gorges

三峡工程

CHINA

Three Gorges Project

Tourism of New Three Gorges

三峡工程

CHINA

Three Gorges Project

Tourism of New Three Gorges

Autumn at Three Gorges

Autumn at Three Gorges

Winter at Three Gorges

三峡工程
CHINA ■

Three Gorges Project

Tourism of New Three Gorges

三峡工程 ■

CHINA

Three Gorges Project

Key Tourist Spots around Three Gorges Reservoir

Ghost Town Scenic Spot (Fengdu Chongqing)

三峡工程

CHINA

Three Gorges Project

Key Tourist Spots around Three Gorges Reservoir

Qu Tang Gorge/Baidi Town Scenic Spot (Fengjie Chongqing)

Small Three Gorges on Daning River (Wushan Chongqing)

三峡工程
CHINA
Three Gorges Project

Key Tourist Spots around Three Gorges Reservoir

Drifting Scenic Spot at Shennongxi Brook (Badong Hubei)

三峡工程
CHINA ■ Three Gorges Project

Key Tourist Spots around Three Gorges Reservoir

三峡工程 ■

Key Tourist Spots around Three Gorges Reservoir

Scenic Spot of Three Gorges Dam (Yichang Hubei)

三峡工程
CHINA
中国 Three Gorges Project

Dachang Town

The Lesser Three Gorges on the Daling River

Shengiongxi River

New Fengjie County

New Wushan County

Bianyu Stream

Scenery in Three Gorges
Reservoir Region

Baidi Town

Goddess peak

Daxi Town

Qingshi

The Heavenly Pit The Earthly Ditch

Shennu Stream

Daling Broad Valley

Wuxia Gorge

Qutang Gorge

Tourist Sketch Map of the Three Gorges

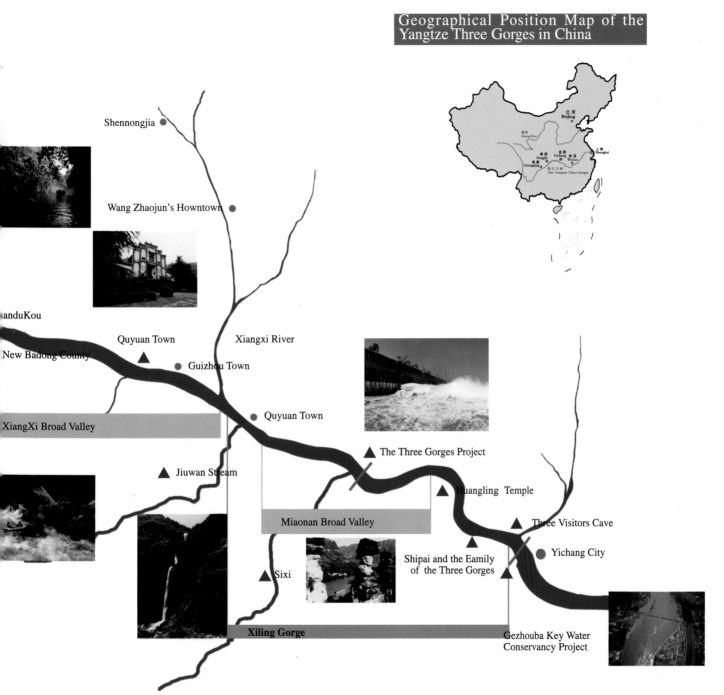

Beijing
北京
Huang River
黄河
Yichang
宜昌
Fengjie
奉节
Wuhan
武汉
Shanghai
上海
Chongqing
重庆
The Yangtze Three Gorges
长江三峡

Shennongjia

Wang Zhaojun's Howntown

anduKou

New Badong County

Quyuan Town

Xiangxi River

Guizhou Town

XiangXi Broad Valley

Quyuan Town

The Three Gorges Project

Jiuwan Stream

Huangling Temple

Miaonan Broad Valley

Three Visitors Cave

Shipai and the Eamily
of the Three Gorges

Yichang City

Sixi

Xiling Gorge

Gezhouba Key Water
Conservancy Project

图书在版编目(CIP)数据

中国长江三峡工程／卢进主编.—武汉：长江出版
社，2006.3
ISBN 7-80708-121-X

Ⅰ.中…   Ⅱ.卢…   Ⅲ.三峡工程—概况—英文
Ⅳ.TV632.71

中国版本图书馆 CIP 数据核字(2006)第 020195 号

主　　编：卢　进

责任编辑：高　伟
装帧设计：朱红霞

摄　　影：卢　进　黄正平　王连生
　　　　　杨铁军　闫　伟　肖佳法
　　　　　徐　洪
翻　　译：深圳市译博士翻译公司
地图绘制：李继宏

出版发行：长江出版社
制版印刷：深圳市精典印务有限公司
开　　本：889mm×1194mm　1/20
印　　张：6.6
版　　次：2006 年 3 月第 1 版第 1 次印刷
发行电话：13907208526
E-mail：X6192@126.com
ISBN 7-80708-121-X/TV.33
定　　价：128.00 元